SHETLAND SHEEPDOG HISTORY

The Shetland Sheepdog came from a group of small, low-lying islands cut by many inlets of the sea and swept by strong winds. Warmed by the Gulf Stream, these islands seldom have much snow, but their climate is generally cold and damp.

Due to the harsh, unarable terrain of the Shetland Islands, sheep farming has thrived for many years, becoming one of Scotland's major industries. Because of the difficulty of the landscape, larger breeds of dog, such as the Collie or the Old English Sheepdog, do not fend well; therefore a small breed of dog such as the Shetland Sheepdog proves more ideal. Shelties are nimble-footed and

In early Sheltie history, the diminutive size of the Shetland Sheepdog was very hard to retain when crossbreeding with small Collies. Today, however, this type of breeding is hardly, if ever, undertaken and greatly discouraged.

graceful, making them capable of maneuvering over rocks and crevices in the terrain. During the 19th century, historians cite references to a bantamized (or miniaturized) Collie type dog that was utilized in the Shetland Islands for tending sheep.

"Toonies," as they have been called, were small farm dogs that arrived in England allegedly from the Shetland Islands. There is no doubt that the English, who like many cultures have favored beautiful things in miniature, would adore these Sheltie ancestors—or Toonies. We are nearly certain that these very dogs are the progenitors of the breed we know and love today—the Shetland Sheepdog.

Before we met the Shetland Sheepdog, we knew of another small purebred: the Shetland Pony. Every child wakes up one morning with dreams of a Shetland Pony on their doorstep. Unfortunately, most children don't get a pony, though many may be equally delighted with a Shetland Sheepdog. He is the best pony substitute ever. Today the breed actually bears the same relationship in size and appearance to the Rough Collie as the Shetland Pony does to an earlier breed of British horse.

Technically, however, the Shetland Sheepdog's resemblance to the rough Collie (that's the Lassie type one, with longer hair, mane and frill) is pronounced to the naked eye, although there are some notable differences between these two recognizable purebreds. It is amazing, however, that many people today still refer to the Sheltie as the "miniature Collie," which most Sheltie people take offense to—and rightly so!

The first showing of these dogs in England precipitated a controversy, for they were known as Shetland Collies. Collies were being sold for fancy prices, and small wonder that the breeders resented the encroachment. A few years later it was agreed that the breed would be known as Shetland Sheepdogs.

As with any new and exciting breed on the horizon, the people breeding the dog have to make decisions about how the dog should look. Too often breeders insist on further miniaturization of the dog, usually resulting in lack of soundness in body and temperament. Fortunately for the Shetland Sheepdog, early breeders decided that the breed should emulate the show Collie. They did not emphasize or insist upon absolute petiteness. In the early 1900s, breeders were looking for soundness instead of extreme smallness.

Around the same time, Shetland Sheepdogs began to

Shetland Sheepdogs are frequently referred to as "Miniature Collies." Although this nomenclature is frowned upon, the relationship between the Collie (shown here) and the Sheltie is still evident.

For a herding dog, alertness and obedience are of prime importance to the safety of the flock, and today these characteristics show plainly. This Sheltie is keeping watch over several Nubian goats.

arrive on American shores. The year was apparently 1911 and various imported dogs were being sold and campaigned on a moderate scale. Americans, quite opposite of their English forbears, have always favored large size over small. Not to say that Americans wouldn't soon take to the Sheltie, but over the course of time, American dogs would be notably larger than English or Scottish dogs. Of course, the Collie had a paw in these larger dogs.

The national parent club in the United States would be the American Shetland Sheepdog Association, which was organized to sponsor the breed here in 1929.

As Americans took on the breed, the pursuit to improve "type" began and the natural tendency with improved type was larger size. Instead of breeding a quality and "typy" Sheltie to the same, breeders relied more on the Collie, thus always battling the ever-increasing size of the dogs. While the Collie itself had many of the classic features trying to be established in Sheltie lines, these smaller Collies were still substantially larger than the Shetland Sheepdogs with whom they were bred.

It is acknowledged then that some Collie crossing was relied upon in the early years, but it became increasingly difficult to avoid throwbacks to Collie size. Today no such breeding goes on (at least in the public eye); additionally, the national registries do not allow outcrosses to Collies. Likewise, the height disqualification in the standard efficiently precludes any oversized dogs from the show ring.

The standard has also done the breed a service in eliminating shyness from the Sheltie, a trait that once haunted the breed in earlier times. Even today there are some dogs which are "shyer" than would be desired, though few flinch or cringe under the hand of their loving owner or an inspecting show judge. Socializing the dogs at an early age has helped immensely in propagating lines of Shelties that readily accept strangers' handling. In all fairness, the history of the breed as a one-man (one-shepherd) dog who rarely contacted other humans has influenced the breed's temperament and the tendency toward shyness. Fortunately, few breeders have a problem in this regard today, and Shelties have become one of the most popular of all home companions.

THE ANCESTORS OF ALL SHELTIES

The original Shetland Collie (from which the Sheltie is derived)

There are several distinct differences between the Sheltie and the Collie, one being the Sheltie's ears said to "be set like a furry pair of wings."

was intermixed with many other breeds before the standard breed of Sheltie appeared. Some Shelties display a saucy, upturned tail. This tail comes from the Icelandic sheepdog, who shares this trait with the Alaskan Husky. The yellowish color seen in some Shelties is apparently a result of blood from the Greenland Yakki. Both the Icelandic and Greenland breeds gave the Shetland Collie his pointed and erect ears.

Legend has it that a yacht that carried a King Charles Spaniel docked at the Shetland Islands when the Sheltie breed was developing. The Spaniel escaped and was kept on the island and traits of this special breed were bred into the Sheltie. The Greenland and Iceland dogs gave the Sheltie his thick coat for protection against the elements. The King Charles Spaniel, on the other hand, gave him his silk-like sheen. Because the King Charles Spaniel had a naturally longer coat than the northern dogs, the Sheltie inherited ticking (flecks of color) on his legs and face. Large round eyes and black-and-tan coloring in the present day Sheltie are also marks of the impudent Spaniel who "jumped ship" many years ago.

By far the most dominant influence in the modern Sheltie comes from the Collie. The Border Collie, especially, seems to be the basis of the Sheltie breed. You can see the Collie influence in your Sheltie by observing the lean head and long muzzle.

THE EARLY SHELTIE

The general appearance of the original Shetland dogs may be learned from a description published in 1906. The average type was described as a Collie in miniature, but the description noted several points of divergence, especially the ears that were set like a pair of furry wings. The body of these early Shetlands was long, set low on sturdy, well-feathered short legs; the usual weight varied from six to ten pounds. The prettier dogs were white or white with gold markings, although black-and-tan or all black were more common. The long, silky coat was rare; the half-long soft coat was more in evidence. The

Although a Sheltie seldom either starts or becomes involved in a fight, he will not hesitate to defend his master or family when the need arises.

eyes were soft, round, and in good proportion to the size of the head.

The early dogs have also been described as resembling the Butterfly dog, or Papillon, of today. They have been likened to the long-haired Chihuahua, originally known as the Mexican Toy Shepherd. This Mexican Toy Shepherd had a heavier muzzle, coarser and larger frame, and a coat like silk floss, having the fringed effect of the Papillon's coat.

The original Shetland Sheepdog was neither sufficiently pure-bred nor of enough real merit upon which to found a show breed without outside help. Reared in the rigorous northern climate, the dogs had lived and worked for many generations under conditions that required unusual stamina, a sturdy build, and a high degree of intelligence. Owing to environmental forces, however, the Shetland dogs that were sent out from the Islands in the beginning were very uneven in type, although they did possess great stamina and fine muscular development.

DESCRIPTION OF THE BREED

Known to all the world as the Sheltie, the Shetland Sheepdog is naturally attentive and protective, given his shepherd ancestry. As a shepherd's dog, keenly aware of his master's needs, the Shetland Sheepdog is able to coordinate a flock by following the shepherd's commands and signals. The Sheltie today possesses all the keen awareness and obedience of his flock-working forebears but combines this loyalty with unwavering devotion and heartfelt affection for his keepers. Of course, the Sheltie's life is much easier today, with no massive flock to guide or rugged terrain to endure day after day. Nevertheless, the Sheltie thrives when given a task to do, a command to obey, a goal to reach. These are very goal-oriented animals who live to heed their owners' beckoning, to please their owners through obedience. Not all breeds of dogs care to obey their masters. The Sheltie's loving willingness to do

True to his shepherding ancestry, today's Sheltie continues to stay close to his master's side.

as you say is an inbred trait. Shepherds many generations ago are responsible for selectively breeding for this highly desirable trait.

The Shepherds also bred for another valuable trait, the desire to stay close to home and master. This protective trait was a priority for a shepherd, since a dog that wandered far from the flock was a major liability. A Sheltie must exhibit great self control and not give in to his every curiosity. The ever-curious Sheltie chasing a passing rabbit or squirrel and leaving his flock is arguably alert, though no advantage to his master. Who would argue, however, that most Shelties today would fail the curiosity test and chase the squirrel? But then again, few Shelties have real flocks to guard, and dogs will be dogs.

The point of the discussion is that Shelties instinctively will stay close to their master. Owners are grateful that their dogs do not run from their side

The Sheltie proves to be a versatile dog: he can be a family pet, a show dog or an obedience worker. He especially excels in households with children.

whenever they drop their leash or open the front gate. This reliability can be counted upon, and also saves many dogs' lives. Many breeds need to be taught to "heel," but somehow the Sheltie instinctively knows the importance of remaining at his master's side and close to his flock, which in today's world is his family.

The Sheltie's herding instincts have not gone completely by the wayside, and Shelties frequently "herd" the family's young children around the yard, especially when they sense the children are getting into mischief. Without realizing it, we take advantage of our Sheltie's natural-born traits, the results from generations of selective breeding by Scottish shepherds, and aren't we glad for most of these remarkable characteristics. . . and how amazingly few of them have to do with actual sheep!

Sheltie owners only a few years ago used to laugh about the fact that their dogs had never even seen a sheep, wouldn't even recognize one of the woolly buggers if they met him in a dark alley. Today our remarkable little non-working Shelties have proven us wrong, happily showing us that not only do they recognize sheep but they can even move a few of them around without any prior experience or instruction. We are talking about Instinct Tests, sponsored by local Shetland Sheepdog clubs and the American Kennel Club. How

surprised Sheltie owners were when their beloved house pets were interacting with livestock and proving surprisingly efficient too.

The Shetland Sheepdog can be rightly described as a dog underfoot, perhaps taking the heeling lesson to the extreme. Most owners confess that their dogs follow them around the house, from room to room, from chore to chore. (Why not involve him in those chores? He will prove amazingly proficient, and fast!) Fortunately the Sheltie instantly knows when he is needed, and he will get out of the way when instructed so, although he'd rather be close and feel needed (like everyone else in the world).

Obedience in a dog is a virtue beyond telling, and the most difficult of all tasks for a dog owner is keeping the dog under control at all times. Aren't we glad that those shepherds taught their dogs to follow hand signals and whistles! That the Sheltie will obey every time is invaluable—and will save his life on many occasions. In traffic, in crowds, or in any strange situation, you have the comfort of knowing your Sheltie will follow your directions to the tee.

Is the Shetland Sheepdog intelligent? Most dogs are intelligent by nature, but studies today have finally recognized that the herding breeds are far and away the smartest of all dogs as a group. If you've ever seen a Sheltie working in conjunction with his master in a pasture or on a hill, you wouldn't question its intelligence. Shelties think! Some would argue that they reason too, actively make decisions after considering the options. Observing a sheepdog reveals illustrations of the dog's waiting, planning and thinking through an operation. Sometimes the dog second-guesses his master—sometimes he's right. These qualities in the present-day breed make for an interesting, lively home coexistence. Shelties quickly adapt to new situations, adjusting to new things and people with remarkable ease.

We understand that the sheepdog, while employed as a herding dog, did not have the responsibility of protecting the flock as much as keeping it together. Usually a larger dog would be used to guard the flock: this dog was the more aggressive and powerful of the shepherd's dogs. In the Shetland Islands, there apparently were few predators that would threaten the well being of the flock. The Sheltie, therefore, was not a fighter and

Sheltie pups are playful and bounding with energy, making them the perfect pets for children.

rarely challenged an opponent. A herding dog that was quarrelsome would be more prone to leave the flock, and that we know is a liability in a sheepdog. Few Shelties ever engage in any confrontations with other dogs. They are not afraid of other dogs just simply uninterested in proving their dominance. Owners of course welcome these characteristics and are glad that they don't have to worry about their dog picking on a passing Pekingese or getting tangled up in the neighborhood's feisty Doberman.

Nonetheless, this is not to imply that the Sheltie will not defend his master or his family when the need arises. Many Shelties have risen to emergencies and performed heroically in the face of danger, including killing snakes and other ill-minded creatures that threaten their master's path. Of course the Sheltie is too small to be a guard-dog, but you can be sure that he will do his very best to protect his family whenever the need arises.

SHETLAND SHEEPDOG STANDARD

General Appearance—-
*Preamble-—*The Shetland Sheepdog, like the Collie, traces to the Border Collie of Scotland, which, transported to the Shetland Islands and crossed with small, intelligent, longhaired breeds, was reduced to miniature proportions. Subsequently crosses were made from time to time with Collies. This breed now bears the same relationship in size and general appearance to the Rough Collie as the Shetland Pony does to some of the larger breeds of horses. Although the resemblance between the Shetland Sheepdog and the Rough Collie is marked, there are differences that may be noted. The Shetland Sheepdog is a small, alert, rough-coated, longhaired working dog. He must be sound, agile and sturdy. The outline should be so symmetrical that no part appears out of proportion to the whole. Dogs should appear masculine; bitches feminine.

Size, Proportion, Substance— The Shetland Sheepdog should stand between 13 and 16 inches at the shoulder. Note: Height is

Before you purchase your Sheltie puppy, compare your prospect against the breed standard. This three-and-a-half-month-old blue merle is standing nicely to show off its attributes.

Shetland Sheepdogs should stand between 13 and 16 inches at the shoulder.

eyes combine to produce expression. Normally the expression should be alert, gentle, intelligent and questioning. Toward strangers the eyes should show watchfulness and reserve, but no fear.

Eyes medium size with dark, almond-shaped rims, set somewhat obliquely in skull. Color must be dark, with blue or merle eyes permissible in blue merles only. *Faults*—Light, round, large or too small. Prominent haws. *Ears* small and flexible, placed high, carried three-fourth erect, with tips breaking forward. When in repose the ears fold lengthwise

determined by a line perpendicular to the ground from the top of the shoulder blades, the dog standing naturally, with forelegs parallel to line of measurement.

Disqualifications—Heights below or above the desired size range are to be disqualified from the show ring.

In overall appearance, the body should appear moderately long as measured from shoulder joint to ischium (rearmost extremity of the pelvic bone), but much of this length is actually due to the proper angulation and breadth of the shoulder and hindquarter, as the back itself should be comparatively short.

Head—The *head* should be refined and its shape, when viewed from top or side, be a long, blunt wedge tapering slightly from ears to nose.

Expression—Contours and chiseling of the head, the shape, set and use of ears, the placement, shape and color of the

The expression of the Shetland Sheepdog is one of the major points to consider when comparing the dog against the standard. It should be alert, gentle, intelligent, and questioning.

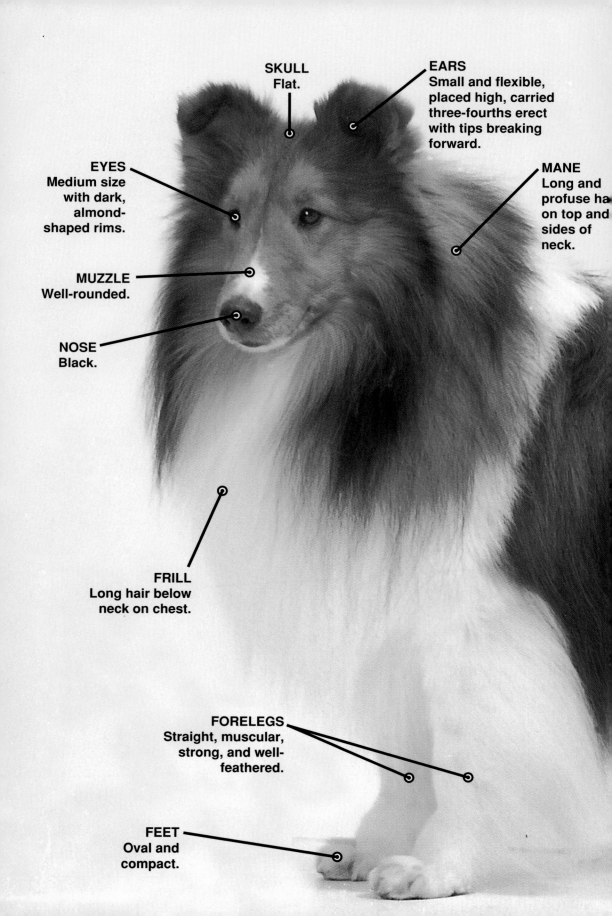

SKULL
Flat.

EARS
Small and flexible, placed high, carried three-fourths erect with tips breaking forward.

EYES
Medium size with dark, almond-shaped rims.

MANE
Long and profuse ha on top and sides of neck.

MUZZLE
Well-rounded.

NOSE
Black.

FRILL
Long hair below neck on chest.

FORELEGS
Straight, muscular, strong, and well-feathered.

FEET
Oval and compact.

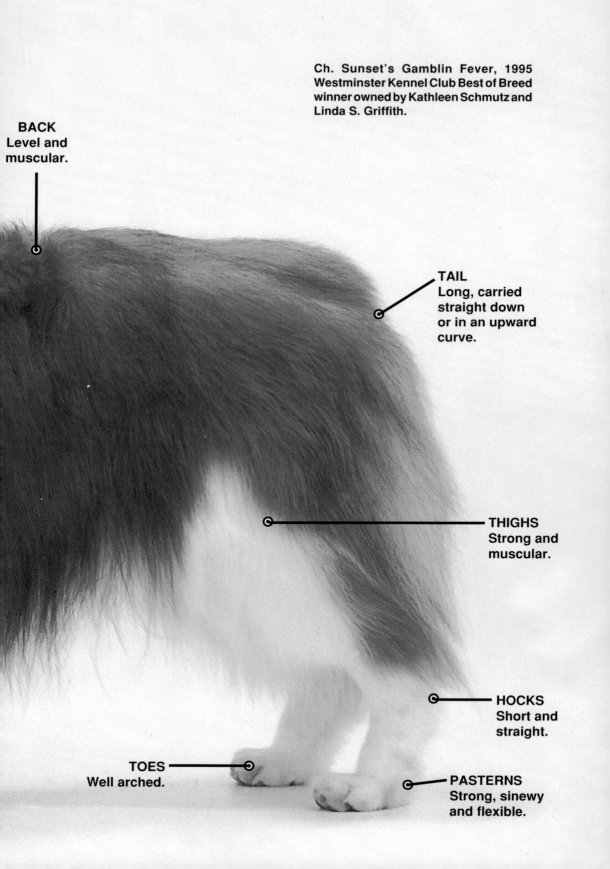

BACK
Level and
muscular.

Ch. Sunset's Gamblin Fever, 1995
Westminster Kennel Club Best of Breed
winner owned by Kathleen Schmutz and
Linda S. Griffith.

TAIL
Long, carried
straight down
or in an upward
curve.

THIGHS
Strong and
muscular.

HOCKS
Short and
straight.

TOES
Well arched.

PASTERNS
Strong, sinewy
and flexible.

and are thrown back into the frill. *Faults*—set too low. Hound, prick, bat, twisted ears. Leather too thick or too thin.

Skull and Muzzle—Top of skull should be flat, showing no prominence at a nuchal crest (the top of the occiput). Cheeks should be flat and should merge smoothly into a well-rounded muzzle. Skull and muzzle should be of equal length, balance point being inner corner of eye. In profile the topline of skull should parallel the top line of muzzle, but on a higher plane due to the presence of a slight but definite stop. Jaws clean and powerful. The deep, well-developed underjaw, rounded at chin, should extend to base of nostril. *Nose* must be black. *Lips* tight. Upper and lower lips must meet and fit smoothly together all the way around. Teeth level and evenly spaced. Scissors *bite*. *Faults*—Too-angled head. Too prominent stop, or no stop. Overfill below, between, or above eyes. Prominent nuchal crest. Domed skull. Prominent cheekbones. Snipy muzzle. Short, receding, or shallow underjaw, lacking breadth and depth. Overshot or undershot, missing or crooked teeth. Teeth visible when mouth is closed.

Neck, Topline, Body—*Neck*

Cocked ears, synonymous with semi-drop or semi-prick, are erect ears in which the tip only is bent forwards. Also known as "tipped ears." Drawing by John Quinn.

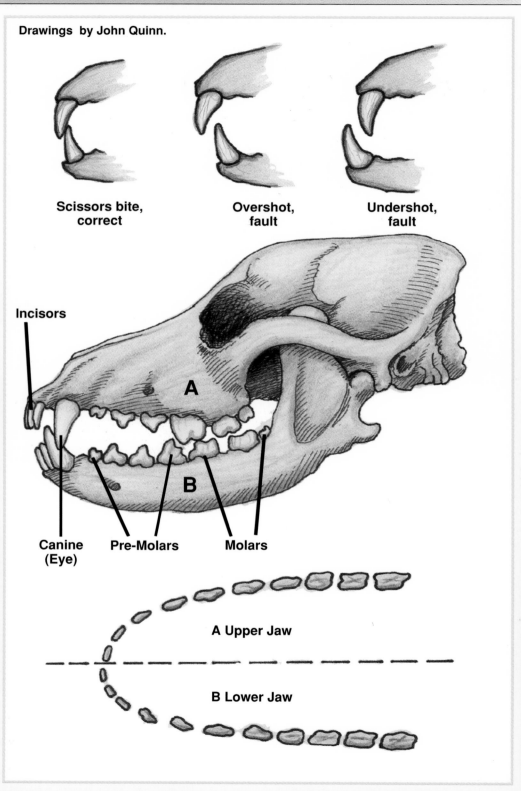

Drawings by John Quinn.

Scissors bite, correct

Overshot, fault

Undershot, fault

Incisors

A

B

Canine (Eye)

Pre-Molars

Molars

A Upper Jaw

B Lower Jaw

A tri-colored Sheltie is a black dog marked with varying amounts of white and tan.

should be muscular, arched, and of sufficient length to carry the head proudly. *Faults—*Too short and thick.

Back should be level and strongly muscled. *Chest* should be deep, the brisket reaching to point of elbow. The ribs should be well sprung, but flattened at their lower half to allow free play of the foreleg and shoulder. Abdomen moderately tucked up. *Faults—*Back too long, too short, swayed or roached. Barrel ribs. Slab-side. Chest narrow and/or too shallow.

There should be a slight arch at the loins, and the *croup* should slope gradually to the rear. The hip-bone (pelvis) should be set at a 30-degree angle to the spine. *Faults—*Croup higher than withers. Croup too straight or too steep.

The *tail* should be sufficiently long so that when it is laid along the back edge of the hind legs the last vertebra will reach the hock joint. Carriage of tail at rest is straight down or in a slight upward curve. When the dog is alert the tail is normally lifted, but it should not be curved forward over the back. *Faults—*Too short. Twisted at end.

Forequarters—From the withers, the shoulder blades

should slope at a 45-degree angle forward and downward to the shoulder joints. At the withers they are separated only the by the vertebra, but they must slope outward sufficiently to accommodate the desired spring of rib. The upper arm should join the shoulder blade at as nearly as possible a right angle. Elbow joint should be equidistant from the ground or from the withers. Forelegs straight viewed from all angles, muscular and clean, and of strong bone. Pasterns very strong, sinewy and flexible. Dewclaws may be removed. *Faults*— Insufficient angulation between shoulder and upper arm. Upper arm too short. Lack of outward slope of shoulders. Loose shoulders. Turning in or out of elbows. Crooked legs. Light bone.

Feet—should be oval and compact with toes well arched and fitting tightly together. Pads deep and tough, nails hard and strong. *Faults*—Feet turning in or out. Splay feet. Hare feet. Cat feet.

Hindquarters—The thigh should be broad and muscular. The thighbone should be set into the pelvis at a right angle of the shoulder blade and upper arm. Stifle bones join the thighbone and should be distinctly angled at the stifle joint. The overall length of the stifle should at least equal the length of the thighbone, and preferably should slightly exceed it. Hock joint should be clean-cut, angular, sinewy, with good bone and strong ligamentation. The hock (metatarsus) should be short and straight viewed from all angles. Dewclaws should be removed. *Faults*—Narrow thighs. Cow-hocks. Hocks turning out. Poorly defined hock point.

Feet as in forequarters.

Coat—the coat should be double, the outer coat consisting of long, straight, harsh hair; the undercoat short, furry, and so dense as to give the entire coat its "standoff" quality. The hair on the face, tips of ears and feet should be smooth. Mane and frill should be abundant, and particularly impressive in males. The forelegs

Shelties are a "coat breed." One of their most beautiful assets is their long, straight, dense coat with its "standoff" quality.

The acceptable colors for the Shetland Sheepdog are black, blue merle and sable with white and/or tan markings.

well feathered, the hind legs heavily so, but smooth below the hock joint. Hair on tail profuse. *Note*: Excess hair on ears, feet and on hocks may be trimmed for the show ring. *Faults*—Coat short or flat, in whole or in part; wavy, curly, soft or silky. Lack of undercoat. Smooth-coated specimens.

Color—Black, blue merle, and sable (ranging from golden through mahogany); marked with varying amounts of white and/or tan. *Faults*—Rustiness in a black or a blue coat. Washed-out or degenerate colors, such as pale sable and faded blue. Self-color in the case of blue merle, that is, without any merling or mottling and generally appearing as a faded or dilute tri-color. Conspicuous white body spots.

Specimens with more than 50 percent white shall be so severely penalized as to effectively eliminate them from competition. *Disqualification*—Brindle.

Gait—The trotting gait of the Shetland Sheepdog should denote effortless speed and smoothness. There should be no jerkiness, nor stiff, stilted, up-and-down movement. The drive should be from the rear, true and straight, dependent upon correct angulation, musculation, and ligamentation of the entire hindquarter, thus allowing the dog to reach well under his body with his hind foot and propel himself forward. Reach of stride of the foreleg is dependent upon correct angulation, musculation and ligamentation of the forequarters, together with correct width of chest and construction of rib cage. The foot should be lifted only enough to clear the ground as the leg swings forward. Viewed from the front, both forelegs and hindlegs should move forward almost perpendicular to ground at the walk, slanting a little inward at a slow trot, until at a swift trot the feet are brought so far inward toward center line of body that the tracks left show two parallel lines of footprints actually touching a center line at their inner edges. *There should be no crossing of the feet or throwing of the weight from side to side.*

Faults—Stiff, short steps, with a choppy, jerky movement. Mincing steps, with a hopping up and down, or a balancing of weight from side to side (often erroneously admired as a "dancing gait" but permissible in young puppies). Lifting of front feet in hackney-like action, resulting in loss of speed and energy. Pacing gait.

Temperament—The Shetland Sheepdog is intensely loyal, affectionate, and responsive to his owner. However, he may be reserved toward strangers but not to the point of showing fear or cringing in the ring. *Faults*— Shyness, timidity, or nervousness. Stubbornness, snappiness, or ill temper.

DISQUALIFICATIONS

Heights below or above the desired size range, i.e. 13-16 inches.

Brindle color.

The movement of a Sheltie should be smooth rather than jerky or prancing, denoting effortless speed.

When choosing your Sheltie puppy, remember that it is a "major investment"; not only is a sizable sum of money involved, but you are assuming responsibility for a living creature for many years. Choose carefully.

YOUR SHELTIE PUPPY

SELECTION

When you do pick out a Shetland Sheepdog puppy as a pet, don't be hasty; the longer you study puppies, the better you will understand them. Make it your transcendent concern to select only one that radiates good health and spirit and is lively on his feet, whose eyes are bright, whose coat shines, and who comes forward eagerly to make and to cultivate your acquaintance. Don't fall for any shy little darling that wants to retreat to his bed or his box, or plays coy behind other puppies or people, or hides his head under your arm or jacket appealing to your protective instinct. *Pick the Shetland Sheepdog puppy who forthrightly picks you! The feeling of attraction should be mutual!*

The moment you start thinking about purchasing a Sheltie puppy, it makes sense to observe as many members of the breed as possible prior to taking the big step. Don't fall for that first cute little puppy you see.

DOCUMENTS

Now, a little paper work is in order. When you purchase a purebred Shetland Sheepdog puppy, you should receive a transfer of ownership, registration material, and other "papers" (a list of the immunization shots, if any, the puppy may have been given; a note on whether or not the puppy has been wormed; a diet and feeding schedule to which the puppy is accustomed) and you are welcomed as a fellow owner to a long, pleasant association with a most lovable pet, and more (news)paper work.

GENERAL PREPARATION

You have chosen to own a particular Shetland Sheepdog puppy. You have chosen it very carefully over all other breeds and all other puppies. So before you ever get that Shetland Sheepdog puppy home, you will have prepared for its arrival by reading everything you can get your hands on having to do with the management of Shetland Sheepdogs and puppies. True, you will run into many conflicting opinions, but at least you will not be starting "blind." Read, study, digest. Talk over your plans with your veterinarian, other

"Shetland Sheepdog people," and the seller of your Shetland Sheepdog puppy.

When you get your Shetland Sheepdog puppy, you will find that your reading and studying are far from finished. You've just scratched the surface in your plan to provide the greatest possible comfort and health for your Shetland Sheepdog; and, by the same token, you do want to assure yourself of the greatest possible enjoyment of this wonderful creature. You must be ready for this puppy mentally as well as in the physical requirements.

The safest means to transport your Sheltie, at any age, is in a crate. This should be just large enough to fit an adult Sheltie comfortably but not too large that he would be jostled around.

TRANSPORTATION

If you take the puppy home by car, protect him from drafts, particularly in cold weather. Wrapped in a towel and carried in the arms or lap of a passenger, the Shetland Sheepdog puppy will usually make the trip without mishap. If the pup starts to drool and to squirm, stop the car for a few minutes. Have newspapers handy in case of car-sickness. A covered carton lined with newspapers provides protection for puppy and car, if you are driving alone. Avoid excitement and unnecessary handling of the puppy on arrival. A Shetland Sheepdog puppy is a very small "package" to be making a complete change of sur-roundings and company, and he needs frequent rest and refreshment to renew his vitality.

THE FIRST DAY AND NIGHT

When your Shetland Sheepdog puppy arrives in your home, put him down on the floor and don't pick him up again, except when it is absolutely necessary. He is a dog, a real dog, and must not be lugged around like a rag doll. Handle him as little as possible, and permit no one to pick him up and baby him. To repeat, *put your Shetland Sheepdog puppy on the floor or the ground and let him stay there except when it may be necessary to do otherwise.*

Quite possibly your Shetland Sheepdog puppy will be afraid for a while in his new surroundings, without his mother and littermates. Comfort him and reassure him, but don't console him. Don't give him the "oh-you-poor-itsy-bitsy-puppy" treatment. Be calm, friendly, and reassuring. Encourage him to walk around and sniff over his new home. If it's dark, put on the lights. Let him roam for a few minutes while you and everyone else concerned sit quietly or go about your routine business. Let the puppy come back to you.

Playmates may cause an immediate problem if the new Shetland Sheepdog puppy is to be greeted by children or other pets. If not, you can skip this subject. The natural affinity between puppies and children calls for some supervision until a live-and-let-live relationship is established. This applies particularly to a Christmas puppy, when there is more excitement than usual and more chance for a puppy to swallow something upsetting. It is a better plan to welcome the puppy several days before or after the holiday week. Like a baby, your Shetland Sheepdog puppy needs much rest and should not be over-handled. Once a child realizes that a puppy has "feelings" similar to his own, and can readily be hurt or injured, the opportunities for play and responsibilities provide exercise and training for both.

For his first night with you, he should be put where he is to sleep every night—say in the kitchen, since its floor can usually be easily cleaned. Let him explore the kitchen to his heart's content;

Young puppies often tucker out in the middle of play. Don't disturb a pup when he's sleeping, no matter how cute he looks!

Your puppy should be semi-housebroken when he leaves the breeder. Most breeders teach their puppies to "puddle" in certain newspaper-lined areas. When housebreaking your Sheltie puppy, take a piece of newspaper that he has "puddled" on and place it in the spot where you would like him to go.

close doors to confine him there. Prepare his food and feed him lightly the first night. Give him a pan with some water in it—not a lot, since most puppies will try to drink the whole pan dry. Give him an old coat or shirt to lie on. Since a coat or shirt will be strong in human scent, he will pick it out to lie on, thus furthering his feeling of security in the room where he has just been fed.

HOUSEBREAKING HELPS

Now, sooner or later—mostly sooner—your new Shetland Sheepdog puppy is going to "puddle" on the floor. First take a newspaper and lay it on the puddle until the urine is soaked up onto the paper. *Save this paper.* Now take a cloth with soap and water, wipe up the floor and dry it well. Then take the wet paper and place it on a fairly large square of newspapers in a convenient corner. When cleaning up, always keep a piece of wet paper on top of the others. Every time he wants to "squat," he will seek out this spot and use the papers. (This routine is rarely necessary for more than three days.) Now leave your Shetland Sheepdog puppy for the night. Quite probably he will cry and howl a bit; some are more stubborn than others on this matter. But let him stay alone for the night. This may seem harsh treatment, but it is the best procedure in the long run. Just let him cry; he will weary of it sooner or later.

EXERCISE AND ENVIRONMENT

Any dog who was expected to "rough" it in the inclement conditions of the Shetland Islands must be of strong constitution. The small Sheltie derives from hardy, strong working dogs and comes to us today as a vigorous, healthy and thriving companion animal.

Would a Sheltie be more happy on a farm than in a Manhattan fifth-floor walk up? Possibly, but the Sheltie's foremost priority is YOU. If you live on a farm or in Greenwich Village, your Sheltie will be content beyond words and

Shelties are always happy to be outside. The Sheltie's profuse and well-insulated coat gives him much resistance to cold weather.

reason. The breed is perfectly able to thrive in any setting. In a rural setting, the Sheltie will find much to do to keep him busy. He is by nature an outdoor dog, though he never wants to spend the night alone outside. If you cannot keep your Sheltie in the house with you, do not choose this breed. A Sheltie kept solely outdoors is an unhappy, barky dog. No Sheltie should ever lead such an existence.

Since Shelties require so little in the way of special care and attention, it seems a crime that any dog need go without. He thrives under almost any conditions, including the city apartment scenario although he is probably most "at home" in the suburbs where he can be with his family day in and day out. A fenced-in property is ideal. Although we know the Sheltie is not a wanderer, fences are safety measures and keep stray dogs from your property. For exercise purposes, the fenced-in yard is every Sheltie's need.

Commonly Shetland Sheepdogs admire children and enjoy their company. Remember that the Sheltie is small, and while he is not the most fragile of companion dogs, he shouldn't be exposed to boisterous, untrained children. Yes, he will tolerate much mishandling, but let's not allow children to treat our Shelties unkindly. Children view dogs as playthings and need to be taught that dogs are not inanimate objects to be yanked and tugged at. Adults must supervise children whenever they are playing with a dog, particularly a puppy. Sheltie puppies are marvelously resilient and seem to thrive on children's attention, since children are kind of "Shetland people," and Shelties feel perfectly sized with them. A mistreated or teased puppy can grow up into a dog that does not like children, and this is undesirable with any dog.

EXERCISE

Since the Shetland Sheepdog is small, he can get quite a lot of exercise bounding about the house, helping his master with the day's chores and busying himself with chores of his own. Shelties don't just live in households, they run them! Shelties are natural supervisors (as was expected of them in their shepherding days). He will watch for the delivery man, the mail man, and the repair man; he keeps track of everyone's schedule, knowing precisely who's due when (and who's late); he does the best of jobs herding the family through their daily routines. Shelties can be quite content homebodies, though they really do need a fair amount of time outdoors. These are active dogs that thrive physically and mentally

when given sufficient outlets for their energies. Running about the yard is great fun for the Sheltie. He loves to watch over the neighborhood and to keep a close eye on the property. Daily walks, however, are par for the course since it gives the Sheltie some structured time with his master. Shetland Sheepdogs should not be neglected of their walks as this is a good time for owner and dog to unwind together, to take care of business, or to just escape the normal domestic routine.

The Sheltie's profuse and well-insulated coat gives him much resistance to cold weather. Although he may look dashing in a sweater, he simply doesn't need one. Given the cold climate of the dog's origin, few climates can make the Sheltie shiver. A dog that spends some of the day outdoors will do well with a draft-free dog house. The house should be warm, with ample bedding and a covering over the entrance. As we know, no Sheltie should be expected to spend the night outdoors: he wants to be inside near you.

Indoors he needs a bed or a crate to call his own. Shelties aren't too fussy about where they snooze, so if your bed is off-limits, you better tell him so while he's a puppy. If not, your bed will be his favorite spot, because it's warm, clean and smells like his favorite person.

Shetland Sheepdogs like to stay dry. They are not puddle walkers and don't like to be out in the rain. Be sure that the dog house is rain-proof or you'll have one damp, unhappy Sheltie.

FEEDING

Now let's talk about feeding your Shetland Sheepdog, a subject so simple that it's amazing there is so much nonsense and misunderstanding about it. Is it expensive to feed a Shetland Sheepdog? No, it is not! You can feed your Shetland Sheepdog economically and keep him in perfect shape the year round, or you can feed him expensively. He'll thrive either way, and let's see why this is true.

First of all, remember a Shetland Sheepdog is a dog. Dogs do not have a high degree of selectivity in their food, and unless you spoil them with great variety (and possibly turn them into poor, "picky" eaters) they will eat almost anything that they become accustomed to. Many dogs flatly refuse to eat nice, fresh beef. They pick around it and eat everything else. But meat—bah! Why? They aren't accustomed to it! They'd eat rabbit fast enough, but they refuse beef because they aren't used to it.

VARIETY NOT NECESSARY

A good general rule of thumb is

Fully weaned puppies need to be fed approximately four times a day until they are about three months old. As they get older, gradually decrease the number of times the puppies eat while increasing the size of the meal.

forget all human preferences and don't give a thought to variety. Choose the right diet for your Shetland Sheepdog and feed it to him day after day, year after year, winter and summer. But what is the right diet?

Hundreds of thousands of dollars have been spent in canine nutrition research. The results are pretty conclusive, so you needn't go into a lot of experimenting with trials of this and that every other week. Research has proven just what your dog needs to eat to keep healthy.

DOG FOOD

There are almost as many right diets as there are dog experts, but the basic diet most often recommended is one that consists of a dry food, either meal or kibble form. There are several of excellent quality, manufactured by reliable companies, research tested, and nationally advertised. They are inexpensive, highly satisfactory, and easily available in stores everywhere in containers of five to 50 pounds. Larger amounts cost less per pound, usually.

If you have a choice of brands, it

Feed your pet Sheltie a good brand food and stick with it. Contents and nutritional values are clearly listed on the labels and careful instructions for feeding are given according to the size and weight of each dog.

is usually safer to choose the better known one; but even so, carefully read the analysis on the package. Do not choose any food in which the protein level is less than 25 percent, and be sure that this protein comes from both animal and vegetable sources. The good dog foods have meat meal, fish meal, liver, and such, plus protein from alfalfa and soy beans, as well as some dried-milk product. Note the vitamin content carefully. See that they are all there in good proportions; and be especially certain that the food contains properly high levels of vitamins A and D, two of the most perishable and important ones. Note the B-complex level, but don't worry about carbohydrate and mineral levels. These substances are plentiful and cheap and not likely to be lacking in a good brand.

The advice given for how to choose a dry food also applies to moist or canned types of dog foods, if you decide to feed one of these.

Having chosen a really good food, feed it to your Shetland Sheepdog as the manufacturer directs. And once you've started,

For no-mess feeding, a feeding tray is very practical. Feeding trays are available in different colors and styles at your local pet shop. Photo courtesy of Penn Plax.

stick to it. Never change if you can possibly help it. A switch from one meal or kibble-type food can usually be made without too much upset; however, a change will almost invariably give you (and your Shetland Sheepdog) some trouble.

WHEN SUPPLEMENTS ARE NEEDED

Now what about supplements of various kinds, mineral and been sick, or is having puppies. Vitamins and minerals are naturally present in all the foods; and to ensure against any loss through processing, they are added in concentrated form to the dog food you use. Except on the advice of your veterinarian, added amounts of vitamins can prove harmful to your Shetland Sheepdog! The same risk goes with minerals.

A Sheltie bitch that is having puppies needs calcium and other supplements added to her diet, otherwise supplements are really not necessary unless your Sheltie has been ill or has been improperly fed.

vitamin, or the various oils? They are all okay to add to your Shetland Sheepdog's food. However, if you are feeding your Shetland Sheepdog a correct diet, and this is easy to do, no supplements are necessary unless your Shetland Sheepdog has been improperly fed, has

FEEDING SCHEDULE

When and how much food to give your Shetland Sheepdog? As to when (except in the instance of puppies), suit yourself. You may feed two meals per day or the same amount in one single feeding, either morning or night. As to how to prepare the food and how much to give, it is generally best to follow the directions on the food package. Your own Shetland Sheepdog may want a little more or a little less.

Fresh, cool water should always be available to your Shetland Sheepdog. This is important to good health throughout his lifetime.

ALL SHETLAND SHEEPDOGS NEED TO CHEW

Puppies and young Shetland Sheepdogs need something with resistance to chew on while their teeth and jaws are developing—for cutting the puppy teeth, to induce growth of the permanent teeth under the puppy teeth, to assist in getting rid of the puppy teeth at the proper time, to help the permanent teeth through the gums, to ensure normal jaw development, and to settle the permanent teeth solidly in the jaws.

The adult Shetland Sheepdog's desire to chew stems from the instinct for tooth cleaning, gum massage, and jaw exercise—plus

The nylon tug toy is actually a dental floss. You grab one end and let your puppy tug on the other as it slowly slips through his teeth since nylon is self-lubricating (slippery). Do not use cotton rope tug toys as cotton is organic and rots. It is also weak and easily loses strands that are indigestible should the puppy swallow them.

the need for an outlet for periodic doggie tensions.

This is why dogs, especially

The Gumabone® Wishbone® and Gumabone® Frisbee®*are excellent chew devices for your Sheltie puppies due to the softer composition. *The trademark Frisbee is used under license from Mattel, Inc., California, USA.

Nylabone® makes many different types of chew toys that will provide your Sheltie with hours of safe entertainment.

things that can be bitten off in chunks, such as from shoes or rubber or plastic toys, may cause an intestinal stoppage (if not regurgitated) and bring painful death, unless surgery is promptly performed.

Strong natural bones, such as 4- to 8-inch lengths of round shin bone from mature beef—either the kind you can get from a butcher or one of the variety available commercially in pet stores—may serve your Shetland Sheepdog's teething needs if his mouth is large enough to handle them effectively.

A scientific study shows a dog's tooth (arrow) while being maintained by Gumabone® chewing.

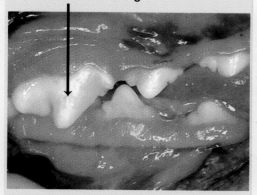

The Gumabone® was taken away and in 30 days the tooth (arrow) was almost completely covered with plaque and tartar.

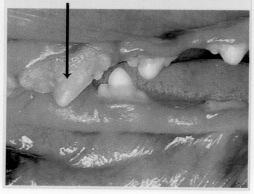

puppies and young dogs, will often destroy property worth hundreds of dollars when their chewing instinct is not diverted from their owner's possessions. And this is why you should provide your Shetland Sheepdog with something to chew—something that has the necessary functional qualities, is desirable from the Shetland Sheepdog's viewpoint, and is safe for him.

It is very important that your Shetland Sheepdog not be permitted to chew on anything he can break or on any indigestible thing from which he can bite sizable chunks. Sharp pieces, such as from a bone which can be broken by a dog, may pierce the intestinal wall and kill. Indigestible

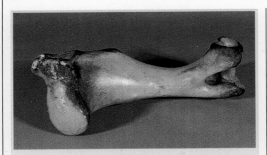

Strong natural beef bones, the kinds that are available only from a butcher or a pet shop, may keep your Sheltie content but are less desirable than nylon or polyurethane bones, which do not damage tooth enamel.

You may be tempted to give your Shetland Sheepdog puppy a smaller bone and he may not be able to break it when you do, but puppies grow rapidly and the power of their jaws constantly increases until maturity. This means that a growing Shetland Sheepdog may break one of the smaller bones at any time, swallow the pieces, and die painfully before you realize what is wrong.

All hard natural bones are very abrasive. If your Shetland Sheepdog is an avid chewer, natural bones may wear away his teeth prematurely; hence, they then should be taken away from your dog when the teething purposes have been served. The badly worn, and usually painful, teeth of many mature dogs can be traced to excessive chewing on natural bones.

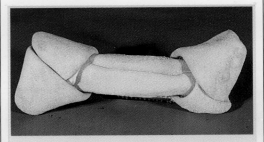

Rawhide is probably the best-selling dog chew. It can be dangerous and cause a dog to choke on it as it swells when wet. A molded, melted rawhide mixed with casein is available (though always scarce).

Contrary to popular belief, knuckle bones that can be chewed up and swallowed by your Shetland Sheepdog provide little, if

Molded rawhide, called Roarhide® by Nylabone®, is very hard and safe for your dog. It is eagerly accepted by Shelties.

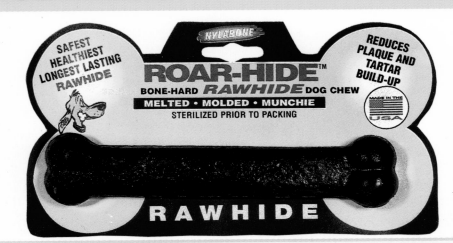

Pet shops sell dog treats which are healthy and nutritious. Cheese is added to chicken meal, rawhide and other high-protein feeds to be melted together and molded into hard chew devices or pacifiers. Don't waste your money on low-protein treats. If the protein content isn't at least 50%, pass it up!

any, usable calcium or other nutriment. They do, however, disturb the digestion of most dogs and cause them to vomit the nourishing food they need.

Dried rawhide products of various types, shapes, sizes, and prices are available on the market and have become quite popular. However, they don't serve the primary chewing functions very well; they are a bit messy when wet from mouthing, and most Shetland Sheepdogs chew them up rather rapidly—but they have been considered safe for dogs until recently. Now, more and more incidents of death, and near death, by strangulation have been reported to be the results of partially swallowed chunks of rawhide swelling in the throat. More recently, some veterinarians have been attributing cases of acute constipation to large pieces of incompletely digested rawhide in the intestine.

A new product, molded rawhide, is very safe. During the process, the rawhide is melted and then injection molded into the familiar dog shape. It is very hard and is eagerly accepted by Shetland Sheepdogs. The melting process also sterilizes the rawhide. Don't confuse this with pressed rawhide, which is nothing more than small strips of rawhide squeezed together.

The nylon bones, especially those with natural meat and bone fractions added, are probably the most complete, safe, and economical answer to the chewing need. Dogs cannot break them or bite off sizable chunks; hence, they are completely safe—and being longer lasting than other things offered for the purpose, they are economical.

Hard chewing raises little bristle-like projections on the surface of the nylon bones—to provide effective interim tooth cleaning and vigorous gum massage, much in the same way your toothbrush does it for you. The little projections are raked off

Chocolate Nylabone® has a one micron thickness coat of chocolate under the skin of the nylon. When the Shetland Sheepdog chews it, the white subsurface is exposed. This photo shows before and after chewing.

Most pet shops have complete walls dedicated to safe pacifiers.

washed in soap and water or it can be sterilized by boiling or in an autoclave.

Nylabone® is highly recommended by veterinarians as a safe, healthy nylon bone that can't splinter or chip. Nylabone® is frizzled by the dog's chewing action, creating a toothbrush-like surface that cleanses the teeth and massages the gums. Nylabone®, the only chew products made of flavor-impregnated solid nylon, are available in your local pet shop. Nylabone® is superior to the cheaper bones because it is made of virgin nylon, which is the strongest and longest-lasting type of nylon available. The cheaper bones are made from recycled or re-ground nylon scraps, and have a tendency to break apart and split easily.

and swallowed in the form of thin shavings, but the chemistry of the nylon is such that they break down in the stomach fluids and pass through without effect.

The toughness of the nylon provides the strong chewing resistance needed for important jaw exercise and effectively aids teething functions, but there is no tooth wear because nylon is non-abrasive. Being inert, nylon does not support the growth of microorganisms; and it can be

Nothing, however, substitutes for periodic professional attention for your Shetland Sheepdog's teeth and gums, not any more than your toothbrush can do that for you. Have your Shetland Sheepdog's teeth cleaned at least once a year by your veterinarian (twice a year is better) and he will be happier, healthier, and far more pleasant to live with.

Raised dental tips on each dog bone work wonders with controlling plaque in Shelties.

Get only the largest Plaque Attacker for your Sheltie.

TRAINING

You owe proper training to your Shetland Sheepdog. The right and privilege of being trained is his birthright; and whether your Shetland Sheepdog is going to be a handsome, well-mannered housedog and companion, a show dog, or whatever possible use he may be put to, the basic training is always the same—all must start with basic obedience, or what might be called "manner training."

Your Shetland Sheepdog must come instantly when called and obey the "Sit" or "Down" command just as fast; he must walk quietly at "Heel," whether on or off lead. He must be mannerly and polite wherever he goes; he must be polite to strangers on the street and in stores. He must be mannerly in the presence of other dogs. He must not bark at children on roller skates, motorcycles, or other domestic animals. And he must be restrained from chasing cats. It is not a dog's inalienable right to chase cats, and he must be reprimanded for it.

Every dog, for its own safety, should learn to recognize and promptly obey the basic commands, "Sit," "Stay," "Come," "No," and "Down." This Sheltie has mastered the "Sit" command.

PROFESSIONAL TRAINING

How do you go about this training? Well, it's a very simple procedure, pretty well standardized by now. First, if you can afford the extra expense, you may send your Shetland Sheepdog to a professional trainer, where in 30 to 60 days he will learn how to be a "good dog." If you enlist the services of a good professional trainer, follow his advice of when to come to see the dog. No, he won't forget you, but too-frequent visits at the wrong time may slow down his training progress. And using a "pro" trainer means that you will have

A properly trained Sheltie will be enjoyed by all family members.

who are also just starting out. You will actually be training your own dog, since all work is done under the direction of a head trainer who will make suggestions to you and also tell you when and how to correct your Shetland Sheepdog's errors. Then, too, working with such a group, your Shetland Sheepdog will learn to get along with other dogs. And, what is more important, he will learn to do exactly what he is told to do, no matter how much confusion there is around him or how great the temptation is to go his own way.

Write to your national kennel club for the location of a training club or class in your locality. Sign up. Go to it regularly—

to go for some training, too, after the trainer feels your Shetland Sheepdog is ready to go home. You will have to learn how your Shetland Sheepdog works, just what to expect of him and how to use what the dog has learned after he is home.

OBEDIENCE TRAINING CLASS

Another way to train your Shetland Sheepdog (many experienced Shetland Sheepdog people think this is the best) is to join an obedience training class right in your own community. There is such a group in nearly every community nowadays. Here you will be working with a group of people

SUCCESSFUL DOG TRAINING is one of the better training books by Hollywood dog trainer Michael Kamer, who trains dogs for movie stars.

Praise and rewards are very important to the proper training of your Shetland Sheepdog.

every session! Go early and leave late! Both you and your Shetland Sheepdog will benefit tremendously.

TRAIN HIM BY THE BOOK

The third way of training your Shetland Sheepdog is by the book. Yes, you can do it this way and do a good job of it too. But in using the book method, select a book, buy it, study it carefully; then study it some more, until the procedures are almost second nature to you. Then start your training. But stay with the book and its advice and exercises. Don't start in and then make up a few rules of your own. If you don't follow the book, you'll get into jams you can't get out of by yourself. If after a few hours of short training sessions your Shetland Sheepdog is still not working as he should, get back to the book for a study session, because it's your fault, not the dog's! The procedures of dog training have been so well systemized that it must be your fault, since literally thousands of fine Shetland Sheepdogs have been trained by the book.

After your Shetland Sheepdog is "letter perfect" under all conditions, then, if you wish, go on to advanced training and trick work.

Your Shetland Sheepdog will love his obedience training, and you'll burst with pride at the finished product! Your Shetland Sheepdog will enjoy life even more, and you'll enjoy your Shetland Sheepdog more. And remember— you *owe good training to your Shetland Sheepdog.*

Lead training your Sheltie should be one of the first things that you teach him. This will make other training sessions, such as heeling, much easier.

SHOWING YOUR SHELTIE

A show Shetland Sheepdog is a comparatively rare thing. He is one out of several litters of puppies. He happens to be born with a degree of physical perfection that closely approximates the standard by which the breed is judged in the show ring. Such a dog should, on maturity, be able to win or approach his championship in

Showing Shetland Sheepdogs is a lot of fun—yes, but it is a highly competitive sport. While all the experts were once beginners, the odds are against a novice. You will be showing against experienced handlers, often people who have devoted a lifetime to breeding, picking the right ones, and then showing those dogs through to their championships. Moreover,

Agility is an obstacle course designed to test a dog's intelligence and coordination. Shelties excel in agility competitions. This Sheltie is perfecting his tire jump.

good, fast company at the larger shows. Upon finishing his championship, he is apt to be as highly desirable as a breeding animal. As a proven stud, he will automatically command a high price for service.

the most perfect Shetland Sheepdog ever born has faults, and in your hands the faults will be far more evident than with the experienced handler who knows how to minimize his Shetland Sheepdog's faults. These are but a

Naturally, when at a show, your Sheltie should look his very best. Probably the single most important step in having your dog look his best is the way in which he was brushed.

few points on the sad side of the picture.

The experienced handler, as I say, was not born knowing the ropes. He learned—*and so can you!* You can if you will put in the same time, study and keen observation that he did. But it will take time!

KEY TO SUCCESS

First, search for a truly fine show prospect. Take the puppy home, raise him by the book, and as carefully as you know how, give him every chance to mature into the Shetland Sheepdog you hoped for. My advice is to keep your dog out of big shows, even Puppy Classes, until he is mature. Maturity in the male is roughly two years; with the female, 14

months or so. When your Shetland Sheepdog is approaching maturity, start out at match shows, and, with this experience for both of you, then go gunning for the big wins at the big shows.

Next step, read the standard by which the Shetland Sheepdog is judged. Study it until you know it by heart. Having done this, and while your puppy is at home (where he should be) growing into a normal, healthy Shetland Sheepdog, go to every dog show you can possibly reach. Sit at the ringside and watch Shetland Sheepdog judging. Keep your ears and eyes open. Do your own

The Puppy Class is the first one in which you should enter your puppy. Puppy Classes are for dogs and bitches that are six to 12 months of age. This pup is being groomed for his debut.

judging, holding each of those dogs against the standard, which you now know by heart.

In your evaluations, don't start looking for faults. Look for the virtues—the best qualities. How does a given Shetland Sheepdog shape up against the standard? Having looked for and noted the virtues, then note the faults and see what prevents a given Shetland Sheepdog from standing correctly or moving well. Weigh these faults against the virtues, since, ideally, every feature of the dog should contribute to the harmonious whole dog.

Judging a show is not an easy task. When making your own notes, look for the best qualities first, and then note the faults. Try to see what prevents a Sheltie from showing well and then weigh this against its virtues. Soon you can be a dog show judge too!

"RINGSIDE JUDGING"

It's a good practice to make notes on each Shetland Sheepdog, always holding the dog against the standard. In "ringside judging," forget your personal preference for this or that feature. What does the standard say about it? Watch carefully as the judge places the dogs in a given class. It is difficult from the ringside always to see why number one was placed over the second dog. Try to follow the judge's reasoning. Later try to talk with the judge after he is finished. Ask him questions as to why he placed certain Shetland Sheepdogs and not others. Listen while the judge explains his placings, and, I'll say right here, any judge worthy of his license should be able to give reasons.

When you're not at the ringside, talk with the fanciers and breeders who have Shetland Sheepdogs. Don't be afraid to ask opinions or say that you don't know. You have a lot of listening to do, and it will help you a great deal and speed up your personal progress if you are a good listener.

THE NATIONAL CLUB

You will find it worthwhile to join the national Shetland Sheepdog club and to subscribe to its magazine. From the national club, you will learn the location of an approved regional club near you. Now, when your young Shetland Sheepdog is eight to ten months old, find out the dates of

Scent discrimination is one of the Utility level events at an obedience trial. The Sheltie is instructed to search for articles that his master has touched.

match shows in your section of the country. These differ from regular shows only in that no championship points are given. These shows are especially designed to launch young dogs (and new handlers) on a show career.

ENTER MATCH SHOWS

With the ring deportment you have watched at big shows firmly in mind and practice, enter your Shetland Sheepdog in as many match shows as you can. When in the ring, you have two jobs. One is to see to it that your Shetland Sheepdog is always being seen to its best advantage. The other job is to keep your eye on the judge to see what he may want you to do next. Watch only the judge and your Shetland Sheepdog. Be quick and be alert; do exactly as the judge directs. Don't speak to him except to answer his questions. If he does something you don't like, don't say so. And don't irritate the judge (and everybody else) by constantly talking and fussing with your dog.

In moving about the ring, remember to keep clear of dogs beside you or in front of you. It is my advice to you *not* to show your Shetland Sheepdog in a regular point show until he is at least close to maturity and after both you and your dog have had time to perfect ring manners and poise in the match shows.

GROOMING

Like almost everything else about the Sheltie, grooming requires little extra attention. This may seem surprising for a breed whose coat is nothing short of glorious. The Shetland Sheepdog is a natural keeper. He can go from early puppyhood through his senior years without ever stepping foot into a grooming salon. But let's not kid ourselves: Shelties shed.

Their abundant undercoat (the soft, downy coat) is shed twice annually and must be groomed daily through the shedding period. If you do not brush him out daily, you will have clumps of cotton and fur coming through his coat (and all over every chair in the house, in the carpet, in the air, etc.). The winter coat is a profuse one and comes in better when helped by a caring, brushing owner. Neglecting a Sheltie's coat, given the potential for such beauty, is a crime, and every owner should take this oath seriously. Let's face it: he's not a big dog, so how much brushing could there be?

Even though your Sheltie's coat is basically "wash and wear," he may need some touch-ups. Many groomers use chalk to whiten the Sheltie's coat. This is frowned upon in the show ring however.

On a regular basis, he'll need a once-over to remove the dead coat from him, but this is true of every dog that has fur. The amount of coat your Sheltie has is based on a few things: environment, genetics and nutrition. If you live in a colder climate, your dog may grow more coat than if he lived in the tropics (though the difference is not as dramatic as you think: if you don't believe me, go to a dog show in Bermuda or Hawaii and see what fabulous coats those dogs have). Genetics affects the coat of a dog in that your dog's parents' and grandparents' coats determine the amount and quality of coat of your dog. Feeding a proper, balanced diet can also promote your dog's good coat. Don't skimp on quality or else you'll see it in your dog's coat. The season can also affect the coat, and your Sheltie should always approach winter with a coat in full bloom.

Once the shedding starts (you don't need a book to tell you when you're Sheltie's "blowing" coat, you will know), use a stiff brush and perhaps a steel-tooth comb to help remove the undercoat. This is best undertaken daily, but every other day is fine if you can stand the "fuzz in the air."

When spring is in the air, so is more of that fuzz. Your Sheltie may "blow" the whole coat in a few days as soon as the hot days less full than in the winter. This is Mother Nature's dress shop at work. Adolescent Shelties during their first couple summers may look truly gangly during this period. Fear not, by his third winter, he'll be gorgeous!

Brushing the coat on a regular basis stimulates the flow of natural oils and spreads it uniformly over the coat. Your

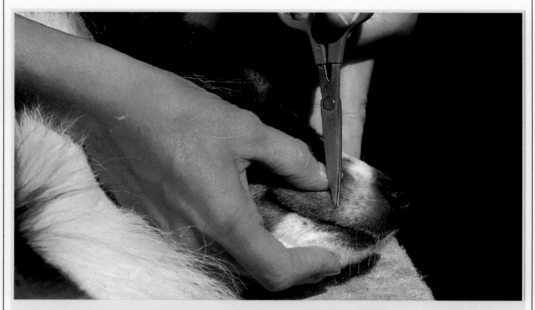

If desired, the facial whiskers of your Sheltie can be removed by snipping them off at the base.

start. We all know that dog days are the hot ones. You can remove clumps of the old coat with a brush, and if you want to give the undercoat a jump-start, give him a hot bath and most of that old coat will come out in a snap. You can brush the coat with a coarse comb twice or thrice a week, within a couple weeks the old coat is gone, making way for a new coat to come in. In the summer his coat will remain smoother and Sheltie will look much more presentable (and be happier too) if he has a well-brushed coat that shows his owner loves him and takes good care of him. It's not unlike seeing a parent out with a child who hasn't been properly bathed and groomed. Our dogs should be our pride—like our children—and not an embarrassment. Dogs should be seen, and always looking their best.

Some Sheltie groomers remove the dog's whiskers. This is completely optional, whether you're showing your dog or not. Perhaps the appearance is neater without the whiskers, but these appendages have utility and probably should not be removed for vanity's sake. In theory the dog's whiskers are intended to (longer hair) along the back of the front legs and the panties should not be trimmed. Of course most groomers will not refrain from removing an unattractive stray long hair to even up the appearance a bit. Ear grooming will depend upon whether the ears are low, erect, or correctly tipped over. Ear carriage is very

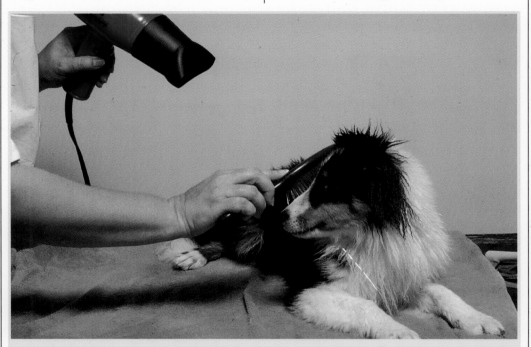

Use a large hairdryer and a good-quality brush after the dog has been bathed. Brushing your Sheltie in the correct manner will add to the apparent fullness of the coat, not to mention keep the hair in a healthy condition.

keep his nose out of trouble. They are admittedly of limited service to the ever-busy Sheltie.

Groomers also trim hair from between the pads of the feet, from the fetlocks, and up the hind legs to the hocks. This gives the foot a neater appearance and also helps prevent any mats from forming. Since the Sheltie should be natural in appearance, feathers important to a Sheltie, just as it is to Collie.

Few Shelties enjoy "natural" ears without a little help. By natural we mean, ears that are carried semi-erect with just the tips folding forward. This ear carriage is quintessential to the expression of the Shetland Sheepdog. Erectness of ears depends upon the strength of a small muscle in the ear and the weight of the ear itself. Not all Shelties are graced with perfect semi-erect ears. Some poor Shelties are cursed with houndlike ears that droop on both sides of their heads, while others have overly perky ears that stick up like a mule's. Both the hound ears and the mule's ears need to be "corrected" for the sake of the Sheltie's expression. The hair on hound ears may be trimmed to get the weight off the ear, while those ears that are sticking straight up may need to be weighted down. Groomers have been fairly creative in what they weight ears down with. Some use petroleum jelly, other big spenders use pennies!

Although many owners will never opt to take a Shetland Sheepdog to a grooming salon, some owners do. Such services such as teeth scaling (to remove plaque and tartar buildup), clipping and filing toenails, etc., are offered at these shops. If you're an owner on the go, or simply aren't inclined to perform these tasks, a grooming salon is an excellent alternative. Remember, *never* allow a groomer

to give your Sheltie a "summer clip." He may never recover! Fortunately groomers these days rarely make such cavalier advances, except perhaps on a crossbreed or mongrel.

While you're grooming the dog, always keep a watchful eye for external parasites, such as fleas and ticks. Pet shops sell fairly effective flea powders that can help in the fight against fleas. As every owner knows, it's an ongoing battle that seemingly never ends. Pet owners, given our modern-day technique, are fighting the good fight against fleas and ticks, but fear not they'll be here long after *Homo Sapiens* are extinct!

There are many different types of dog brushes. Consult your local pet shop dealer for the one that best suits your dog. Photo courtesy of the Kong Company.

Shelties rarely need baths (unless you want to speed up the shedding process). They stay pretty clean and it is uncommon for any substance to get passed the dog's undercoat. If you live in a city where the neighborhood and park are dirty, a periodic bath is probably in order. Some Shelties go their whole lives without a bath, others are bathed on weekends before dog shows. The option is yours. Dogs don't sweat like humans sweat, and dogs don't have human skin which tolerates frequent exposure to water. (We already know that Shelties are a far cry from water dogs!) A show dog is given a bath before most shows (unless of course he's about to blow every hair and you don't want him to look bald in the show ring). Otherwise, Shelties, unless cemented in mud, splattered in skunk, or bunked by city gunk, do always be redolent of mud, skunk or city gunk! Use a good lather of a mild dog shampoo and rinse off with warm water thoroughly. Always use soaps and shampoos and conditioners designed for dogs. These are available at pet shops or pet-supply houses. Do not use human products as they are not balanced for the dog's skin and could cause irritation.

Your Sheltie's teeth will profit from regular brushing. Accustom him to this procedure as a young pup so that he accepts this attention as an adult.

not need to see the inside of a bathtub.

If you must undertake giving your Sheltie a bath, use a tub filled with about 2 or 3 inches of warm (not hot) water, dipping or sponging it over him. Don't try to plunge him into 14 inches of water in the tub or you'll have a crazed and uncooperative Sheltie that will

Rinsing is simple but oh, so important! Soap left in a Sheltie's coat can cause irritation and infection. Use a hose or a dipper, replenishing the tub with clean water as needed. Washing and rinsing his head and around his eyes should be left for last. Don't douse him too enthusiastically—he's probably not having fun, so go easy.

YOUR SHELTIE'S HEALTH

We know our pets, their moods and habits, and therefore we can recognize when our Shetland Sheepdog is experiencing an off-day. Signs of sickness can be very obvious or very subtle. As any mother can attest, diagnosing and treating an ailment require common sense, knowing when to seek home remedies and when to visit your doctor...or veterinarian, as the case may be.

Your veterinarian, we know, is your Shetland Sheepdog's best friend, next to you. It will pay to be choosy about your veterinarian. Talk to dog-owning friends whom you respect. Visit more than one vet before you make a lifelong choice. Trust your instincts. Find a knowledgeable, compassionate vet who knows Shetland Sheepdogs and likes them.

Grooming for good health makes good sense. The Sheltie's coat is double and medium in length. The dense outer coat benefits from regular brushing to keep looking glossy and clean. Brushing stimulates the natural oils in the coat and also removes dead haircoat. Shelties shed seasonally, which means their undercoat (the soft downy white fur) is pushed out by the incoming new coat. A medium-strength bristle brush is all that is required to groom this beautiful breed of dog.

It is to your puppy's best interest that you inquire about the health of its parents and grandparents. Ask for screening certificates from congenital disease registries, such as OFA or CERF.

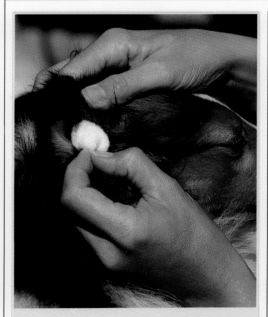

You can clean your Sheltie's ears with a cotton ball dipped in hydrogen peroxide. Be sure not to go deep into the ear canal, only wipe the outer portion.

Occasionally their secretion becomes thickened and accumulates so you can readily feel these structures from the outside. If your Shetland Sheepdog is scooting across the floor dragging his rear quarters, or licking his rear, his anal sacs may need to be expressed. Placing pressure in and up towards the anus, while holding the tail, is the general routine. Anal sac secretions are characteristically foul-smelling, and you could get squirted if not careful. Veterinarians can take care of this during regular visits and demonstrate the cleanest method.

Many Shetland Sheepdogs are predisposed to certain congenital and inherited abnormalities, such as hip dysplasia, the most

The importance of grooming a Sheltie cannot be underestimated. This little dog has a lot of coat and will benefit from daily brushing to avoid matting. Likewise, skin problems in the Sheltie are on the rise, and the breed is prone to demodicosis, also known as red mange.

The Sheltie may also be prone to nasal solar dermatitis, also known as "Collie nose" and pemphigus, an autoimmune diesease which affects the epidermis, sometimes causing a crusting condition (pemphigus foliaceous).

Anal sacs, sometimes called anal glands, are located in the musculature of the anal ring, one on either side. Each empties into the rectum via a small duct.

As a Sheltie owner, you will be able to tell when your pup is not feeling up to par. If things do not seem right, do not hesitate to call your veterinarian.

common hereditary defect in purebred dogs. While there have been many cases, the Shetland Sheepdog does not suffer from a high percentage rate of hip dysplasia thanks to the efforts of conscientious breeders. Nevertheless, new owners must ask for screening certificates from such hip registries as OFA or PennHIP. Since HD is hereditary, it's necessary to know that the parents and grandparents of your puppy had hips rated good or

The undisputed champion of dog health books is Dr. Lowell Ackerman's encyclopedic work *Owner's Guide to DOG HEALTH*. It covers every subject that any dog owner might need. It actually is a complete veterinarian's handbook in simple, easy-to-understand language.

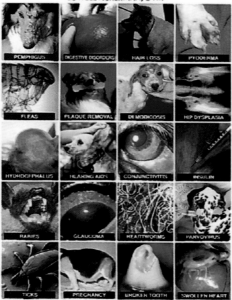

better. Dysplastic dogs suffer from badly constructed hip joints which become arthritic and very painful, thereby hindering the dog's ability to be a working dog, a good-moving show dog, or even a happy, active pet.

Eye conditions such as cataracts, ectasia syndrome, trichiasis and progressive retinal atrophy (PRA) have become concerns for Sheltie breeders. Screening for eye problems has therefore been prioritized. Bilateral cataracts are the most frequently seen in Shetland Sheepdogs, and PRA is an inherited defect that can severely reduce a dog's vision.

Von Willebrand's disease, a bleeding disorder, and Hemophilia A are conditions that affect many dog breeds and do not exclude the Shetland Sheepdog.

Thyroid deficiency can be linked to many symptoms in Shelties, such as obesity, lethargy, and reproductive disorders. Supplementation of the thyroid decreases problems, though such dogs should likely not be bred.

Epilepsy, a possible hereditary condition that is linked to the brain's receiving incorrect stimulus, hinders many breeds of dog and is problematic in Shelties. Affected dogs show signs of mild seizures between six months and three years. Although uncurable, fits can be treated with medication.

Proper care and education can only help owners promote the

Today, Sheltie breeders are very conscientious about the continued health of the breed. Selective breedings take place in which both the dog and bitch have been thoroughly checked for diseases such as hip dysplasia, PRA, von Willebrand's disease, thyroid deficiency and epilepsy.

health and longevity of their Shelties. For the continued health of your dog, owners must attend to vaccinations regularly. Your veterinarian can recommend a vaccination schedule appropriate for your dog, taking into consideration the factors of climate and geography. The basic vaccinations to protect your dog are: parvovirus, distemper, hepatitis, leptospirosis, adenovirus, parainfluenza, coronavirus, bordetella, tracheobronchitis (kennel cough), Lyme disease and rabies.

Parvovirus is highly contagious, dog-specific disease, first recognized in 1978. Targeting the small intestine, parvo affects the stomach, and diarrhea and vomiting (with blood) are clinical signs. Although the dog can pass the infection to other dogs within three days of infection, the initial signs, which include lethargy and depression, don't display themselves until four to seven days. When affecting puppies under four weeks of age, the heart muscle is frequently attacked. When the heart is affected, the puppies exhibit difficulty in breathing and experience crying and foaming at the nose and mouth.

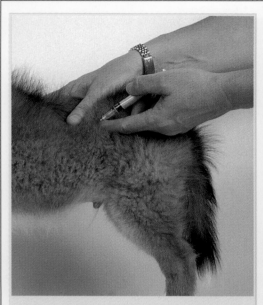

Certain inoculations are given to your puppy and adult dog in the muscle of the back leg, while others are given at the neck.

Distemper, related to human measles, is an airborne virus that spreads in the blood and ultimately in the nervous system and epithelial tissues. Young dogs or dogs with weak immune systems can develop encephalomyelitis (brain disease) from the distemper infection. Such dogs experience seizures, general weakness and rigidity, as well as "hardpad". Since distemper is largely uncurable, prevention through vaccination is vitally important. Puppies should be vaccinated at six to eight weeks of age, with boosters at ten to 12 weeks. Older puppies (16 weeks and older) who are unvaccinated should receive no fewer than two vaccinations at three- to four-week intervals.

Hepatitis mainly affects the liver and is caused by canine adenovirus type I. Highly infectious, hepatitis often affects dogs nine to 12 months of age. Initially the virus localizes in the dog's tonsils and then disperses to the liver, kidney and eyes. Generally speaking the dog's immune system is capable of combating this virus. Canine infectious hepatitis affects dogs whose systems cannot fight off the adenovirus. Affected dogs have fever, abdominal pains, bruising on mucous membranes and gums, and experiences coma and convulsions. Prevention of hepatitis exists only through vaccination at eight to ten weeks of age and then boosters three or four weeks later, then annually.

Leptospirosis is a bacterium-related disease, often spread by rodents. The organisms that spread leptospirosis enter through the mucous membranes

Puppies require a series of shots until they are 12 weeks old, at which time they will begin an annual program.

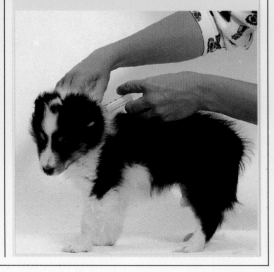

and spread to the internal organs via the bloodstream. It can be passed through the dog's urine. Leptospirosis does not affect young dogs as consistently as the other viruses; it is reportedly regional in distribution and somewhat dependent on the immunostatus of the dog. Fever, inappetence, vomiting, dehydration, hemorrhage, kidney and eye disease can result in moderate cases.

Bordetella, called canine cough, causes a persistent hacking cough in dogs and is very contagious. Bordetella involves a virus and a bacteria: parainfluenza is the most common virus implicated; Bordetella bronchiseptica, the bacterium. Bronchitis and pneumonia result in less than 20 percent of the

Check your dog thoroughly for fleas and ticks when he comes in from the outdoors. Ticks are usually found in heavily treed areas.

cases, and most dogs recover from the condition within a week to four weeks. Non-prescription medicines can help relieve the hacking cough, though nothing can cure the condition before it's run its course. Vaccination cannot guarantee protection from canine cough, but it does ward off the most common virus responsible for the condition.

Lyme disease (also called borreliosis), although known for decades, was only first diagnosed in dogs in 1984. Lyme disease can affect cats, cattle, and horses, but especially people. In the U.S., the disease is transmitted by two ticks carrying the Borrelia burgdorferi organism: the deer tick (Ixodes scapularis) and the western black-legged tick (Ixodes pacificus), the latter primarily affects reptiles. In Europe, Ixodes ricinus is responsible for spreading Lyme. The disease causes lameness, fever, joint swelling, inappetence, and lethargy. Removal of ticks from the dog's coat can help reduce the chances of Lyme, though not as much as avoiding heavily wooded areas where the dog is most likely to contract ticks. A vaccination is available, though it has not been proven to protect dogs from all strains of the organism that cause the disease.

Rabies is passed to dogs and people through wildlife: in North America, principally through the skunk, fox and raccoon; the bat is not the culprit it was once thought to be. Likewise, the common image of the rabid dog foaming at the mouth with every hair on end is unlikely the truest scenario. A rabid dog exhibits difficulty eating, salivates much and has spells of paralysis and awkwardness. Before a dog

Although rabies is on the decline in the world community, tens of thousands of humans die each year from rabies-related incidents.

Parasites have clung to our pets for centuries. Despite our modern efforts, fleas still pester our pet's existence, and our own. All dogs

If introduced at a young age to the family cat, Shelties will usually accept it as a playmate. This Sheltie is three months old and more than fond of his feline companion.

reaches this final state, it may experience anxiety, personality changes, irritability and more aggressiveness than is usual. Vaccinations are strongly recommended as rabid dogs are too dangerous to manage and are commonly euthanized. Puppies are generally vaccinated at 12 weeks of age, and then annually.

itch, and fleas can make even the happiest dog a miserable, scabby mess. The loss of hair and habitual biting and chewing at themselves rank among the annoyances; the nuisances include the passing of tapeworms and the whole family's itching through the summer months. A full range of flea-control and elimination products are available at pet shops, and your veterinarian surely has recommendations. Sprays, powders, collars and dips fight fleas from the outside; drops and pills fight the good fight from inside. Discuss the possibilities with your vet. Not all products can be used in conjunction with one another, and some dogs may be more sensitive to certain applications than others. The dog's living quarters must be debugged as well as the dog itself. Heavy infestation may require multiple treatment.

Always check your dog for ticks carefully. Although fleas can be acquired almost anywhere, ticks are more likely to be picked up in heavily treed areas, pastures or other outside grounds (such as dog shows or obedience or field trials). Athletic, active, and hunting dogs are the most likely subjects, though any passing dog can be the host. Remember Lyme disease is passed by tick infestation.

As for internal parasites, worms are potentially dangerous for dogs and people. Roundworms, hookworms, whipworms, tapeworms, and heartworms comprise the blightsome party of troublemakers. Deworming puppies begins at around two to three weeks and continues until three months of age. Proper

S...
w...   ...that they should be treated
                                        ...onment too!

A healthy litter of puppies. Deworming puppies begins at around two to three weeks and continues until three months of age.

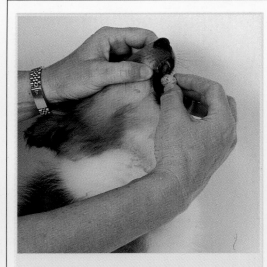

Heartworm preventatives are given orally on a monthly basis. Ivermectin, the active ingredient in most preventatives, has proven very dangerous to Collies, so consult your vet before using such products.

hygienic care of the environment is also important to prevent contamination with roundworm and hookworm eggs. Heartworm preventatives are recommended by most veterinarians, although there are some drawbacks to the regular introduction of poisons into our dogs' system. These daily or monthly preparations also help regulate most other worms as well. Discuss worming procedures with your veterinarian.

Roundworms pose a great threat to dogs and people. They are found in the intestine of dogs, and can be passed to people through ingestion of feces-contaminated dirt. Roundworm infection can be prevented by not walking dogs in heavy-traffic people areas, by burning feces,

Roundworms are typically passed from the bitch to the litter. Your veterinarian can check for these and, if necessary, a deworming procedure can be prescribed.

Supervise your Shelties when they are outdoors at all times. Disease-causing parasites may be ingested from eating off the ground in unhygienic areas.

and by curbing dogs in a responsible manner. (Of course, in most areas of the country, curbing dogs is the law.) Roundworms are typically passed from the bitch to the litter, and bitches should be treated along with the puppies, even if she tested negative prior to whelping. Generally puppies are treated every two weeks until two months of age.

Hookworms, like roundworms, are also a danger to dogs and people. The hookworm parasite (known as Ancylostoma caninum) causes cutaneous larva migrans in people. The eggs of hookworms are passed in feces and become infective in shady, sandy areas. The larvae penetrate the skin of the dog, and the dog subsequently becomes infected. When swallowed, these parasites affect the intestines, lungs, windpipe, and the whole digestive system.

If your Sheltie only rides in the car to go to the veterinarian, he will surely begin to put up a struggle. It is good to take him to a few places that he enjoys so that he does not dread every auto excursion.

Infected dogs suffer from anemia and lose large amounts of blood in the places where the worms latch onto the dog's intestines, etc.

Although infrequently passed to humans, whipworms are cited as one of the most common parasites in America. These elongated worms

Tapeworms are carried by fleas, and enter the dog when the dog swallows the flea. Humans can acquire tapeworms in the same way, though we are less likely to swallow fleas than dogs are. Recent studies have shown that certain rodents and wild animals have been infected with

Proper hygienic care of outdoor grounds is critical in the avoidance of harmful parasites. Water should be supplied to your dogs and cleaned regularly.

affect the intestines of the dog, where they latch on, and cause colic upset or diarrhea. Unless identified in stools passed, whipworms are difficult to diagnose. Adult worms can be eliminated more consistently than the larvae, since whipworms exhibit unusual life cycles. Proper hygienic care of outdoor grounds is critical to the avoidance of these harmful parasites.

tapeworms, and dogs can be affected by catching and/or eating these other animals. Of course, outdoor hunting dogs and terriers are more likely to be infected in this way than are your typical house dog or non-motivated hound. Treatment for tapeworm has proven very effective, and infected dogs do not show great discomfort or symptoms. When people are infected, however, the

Grassy areas are prime breeding grounds for fleas. Brush your Sheltie after romps through such areas to avoid the occurrence.

liver can be seriously damaged. Proper cleanliness is the best bet against tapeworms.

Heartworm disease is transmitted by mosquitoes and badly affects the lungs, heart and blood vessels of dogs. The larvae of Dirofilaria immitis enters the dog's bloodstream when bitten by

has been effective but can be dangerous also. Prevention as always is the desirable alternative. Sheltie owners must beware. Ivermectin is the active ingredient in most heartworm preventatives and has proven very dangerous to Collies. Most veterinarians advise absolute

Sheltie owners typically become "lifers"—they will always and only have Shelties. Considering the breed's minimal requirements and your maximum return, it's easy to see why Sheltie people are as devoted as their dogs.

an infected mosquito. The larvae takes about six months to mature. Infected dogs suffer from weight loss, appetite loss, chronic coughing and general fatigue. Not all affected dogs show signs of illness right away, and carrier dogs may be affected for years before clinical signs appear. Treatment of heartworm disease

caution with Shelties, given the Collie-like nature of the breed. Check with your veterinarian for the preparation best for your dog. Dogs generally begin taking the preventatives at eight months of age and continue to do so throughout the non-winter months.

SUGGESTED READING

The following books are all published by T.F.H. Publications, Inc. and are recommended to you for additional information:

The Book of the Shetland Sheepdog (H-1064) proves to be the most extensive work ever on the breed. Written by proclaimed author and judge, Anna Katherine Nicholas. The most famous Shetland Sheepdogs in the United States, Canada, and Australia along with their beginnings in these countries are brilliantly outlined for the reader. Also included are specific chapters to help one choose a puppy or adult, and then in detail explains how to care for, groom, show, breed and teach obedience. New Shetland Sheepdog owners as well as professionals of the fancy cannot do without this book. Beautifully illustrated with black and white photos throughout, line drawings and spectacular full-color photos. A necessity in any Sheltie home and valued reference guide.

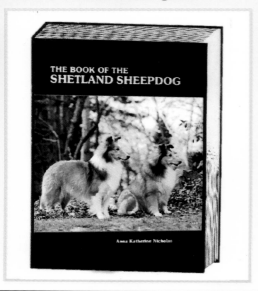

Everybody Can Train Their Own Dog by Angela White (TW-113) is a fabulous reference guide for all dog owners. This well written, easy-to-understand book covers all training topics in alphabetical order for instant location. In addition to teaching, this book provides problem solving and problem prevention techniques that are fundamental to training. All teaching methods are based on motivation and kindness, which bring out the best of a dog's natural ability and instinct.

Owners Guide to Dog Health by Lowell Ackerman, D.V.M. (TS-214) is the most comprehensive volume on dog health available today. Internationally respected veterinarian Dr. Lowell Ackerman examines in full detail the signs of illness and disease, diagnosis treatment and therapy options as well as preventative measures, all in simple terms that are easy for the reader to understand. Hundreds of color photographs and illustrations throughout the text help explain the latest procedures and technological advances in all areas of canine care, including nutrition, skin and haircoat care, vaccinations and more. *Owners Guide to Dog Health* is an absolute must for those who sincerely care about the health of their dog.

Dog Breeding for Professionals by Dr. Herbert Richards (H-969) is a straightforward discussion of how to breed dogs of various sizes and how to care for newborn puppies. The many aspects of breeding (including possible problems and practical solutions) are covered in great detail. *Warning: the explicit photos of canine sexual activities may offend some readers.*

The Atlas of Dog Breeds of the World (H-1091) by Bonnie Wilcox, DVM, and Chris Walkowicz traces the history and highlights the characteristics, appearance and function of every recognized dog breed in the world. 409 different breeds receive full-color treatment and individual study. Hundreds of breeds in addition to those recognized by the American Kennel Club and the Kennel Club

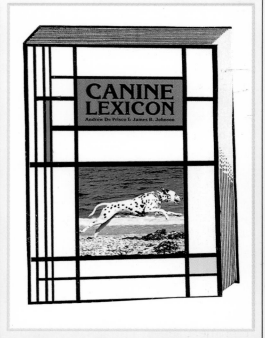

of Great Britain are included— the dogs of the world complete! The ultimate reference work, comprehensive coverage, intelligent and delightful discussions. The perfect gift book.

Canine Lexicon by Andrew De Prisco and James Johnson, (TS-175) is an up-to-date encyclopedic dictionary for the dog person. It is the most complete single volume on the dog ever published covering more breeds than any other book as well as other relevant topics, including health, showing, training, breeding, anatomy, veterinary terms, and much more. No dog book before has ever offered this many stunning color photographs of all breeds, dog sports, and topics (over 1300 in full color).

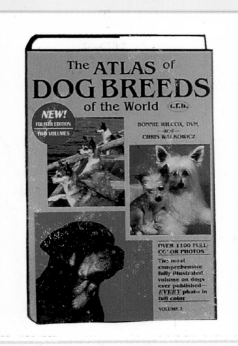